E-POCKET
MEETING

RAY R.

Run an AA meeting like an old-timer, whether you are or not. E-Pocket Meeting is the solution. With E-Pocket Meeting on your phone or tablet, you will be ready to hold an AA meeting.

AA meetings will seem easy whether it is two or three gathered together or a room full of eager newcomers. Another dose of recovery is delivered for another day's sobriety.

Contents

Dedication

To the thousands of men and women who have gone before me, my sincere and heartfelt gratitude. To the group that seemed to grow up around me, thank you for carrying me through those days that I could not carry myself. To my family, near and far, who are the joys of my life, especially my brother Mark who is such a gift. Last, my bride, who has made the life we lead possible by allowing me to keep my program in the forefront of our life.

Introduction

Setting the stage

The E-Pocket Meeting will help those recovering from alcoholism to run an AA meeting. Meetings are one of the keys to success in recovery. But the day comes when it is up to you to run a meeting with none of the regular documents at hand. E-Pocket Meeting is the solution. With E-Pocket Meeting on your phone, or tablet. You will be ready, at a moment's notice, with the basic material to open, run and close an AA meeting like an old-timer.

There are as many ways to run a meeting as there are alcoholics in recovery, E-Pocket Meeting has you covered with enough variations and suggestions to be perfect for most folks comfortable for the rest. With E-Pocket Meeting on your phone or tablet, running an AA meeting will seem easy whether it is two or three gathered together or a room full of eager newcomers. Another dose of recovery is delivered for another day's sobriety.

Note for the printed version: This printed version is for the few folks who can't or won't do e-books. It is missing features that the e-book has. But, it's pretty.

Origin

Everything in this booklet
is from these origins

My own writing during my sobriety, including word-smithing things I have heard in meetings and formats I have used and the book <u>Alcoholics Anonymous</u> copyright text attributed to author with the disclaimer required by the author.

Permission to reprint The AA Grapevine, Inc., copyrighted material in the E-Pocket Meeting does not in any way imply affiliation with or endorsement by either Alcoholics Anonymous or The AA Grapevine, Inc.

The Meeting Format

This is a format to run a recovery meeting with some variations that may work better for you and yours. Use highlights and notes to adjust it as needed for you and your fellowship. There are specifics below.

- Open the meeting with a prayer of your choice, often the 'Serenity Prayer'

- Read 'AA Preamble'

- Read 'How It Works'

- If it is a regular meeting you may want to read the 'Twelve Traditions' occasionally, maybe once a month or right now.

- Ask if anyone has wants to celebrate a milestone or birthday.

- The leader shares on a topic related to recovery from alcoholism such as something from the Big Book

- Using one method or another, pass the sharing around the room

  - Waiting for someone to open up and share

  - Tag where the person sharing picks the next

  - (with and without further instructions like alternating genders, or only someone you don't know)

  - Leader chooses every person who shares or just the first few

  - This list is another ad-infinitum

- <u>Five or so minutes before the meeting plans to end</u>

- Wrap up sharing, maybe ask, "Does anyone have a burning desire?"

- Pass the basket or suggest a method of donating to recovery that suits your area. This could be AAWS or your local intergroup or just enough to pay rent for your space

- Read '<u>A Vision for You</u>' or '<u>The Promises</u>'

- Close with the same <u>prayer</u> you started with or a different prayer

AA Preamble

Often read at, or near,
the beginning of the meeting

Alcoholics Anonymous is a fellowship of men and women who share their experience, strength and hope with each other that they may solve their common problem and help others to recover from alcoholism

The only requirement for membership is a desire to stop drinking. There are no dues or fees for A.A. membership; we are self-supporting through our own contributions. A.A. is not allied with any sect, denomination, politics, organization or institution; does not wish to engage in any controversy; neither endorses nor opposes any causes. Our primary purpose is to stay sober and help other alcoholics to achieve sobriety.

Reprinted with permission

How It Works

Often read at the beginning of the meeting.
The beginning of <u>Alcoholics Anonymous</u>
Chapter Five

Rarely have we seen a person fail who has thoroughly followed our path. Those who do not recover are people who cannot or will not completely give themselves to this simple program, usually men and women who are constitutionally incapable of being honest with themselves.

There are such unfortunates. They are not at fault; they seem to have been born that way. They are naturally incapable of grasping and developing a manner of living which demands rigorous honesty. Their chances are less than average. There are those, too, who suffer from grave emotional and mental disorders, but many of them do recover if they have the capacity to be honest.

Our stories disclose in a general way what we used to be like, what happened, and what we are like now. If you have decided you want what we have and are willing to go to any length to get it--then you are ready to take certain steps.

At some of these we balked. We thought we could find an easier, softer way. But we could not. With all the earnestness at our command, we beg of you to be fearless and thorough from the very start. Some of us have tried to hold on to our old ideas and the result was nil until we let go absolutely.

Remember that we deal with alcohol--cunning, baffling, powerful! Without help it is too much for us. But there is One who has all power--that One is God. May you find Him now!

Half measures availed us nothing. We stood at the turning point. We asked His protection and care with complete abandon. Here are the steps we took, which are suggested as a program of recovery:

1. We admitted we were powerless over alcohol- that our lives had become unmanageable.

2. Came to believe that a Power greater than ourselves could restore us to sanity.

3. Made a decision to turn our will and our lives over to the care of God as we understood Him.

4. Made a searching and fearless moral inventory of ourselves.

5. Admitted to God, to ourselves and to another human being the exact nature of our wrongs.

6. Were entirely ready to have God remove all these defects of character.

7. Humbly asked Him to remove our shortcomings.

8. Made a list of all persons we had harmed, and became willing to make amends to them all.

9. Made direct amends to such people wherever possible, except when to do so would injure them or others.

10. Continued to take personal inventory and when we were wrong promptly admitted it.

11. Sought through prayer and meditation to improve our conscious contact with God as we understood Him, praying only for knowledge of His will for us and the power to carry that out.

12. Having had a spiritual awakening as the result of these steps, we tried to carry this message to alcoholics and to practice these principles in all our affairs.

Many of us exclaimed, "What an order! I can't go through with it."

Do not be discouraged. No one among us has been able to maintain anything like perfect adherence to these principles. We are not saints. The point is that we are willing to grow along spiritual lines. The principles we have set down are guides to progress. We claim spiritual progress rather than spiritual perfection.

Our description of the alcoholic, the chapter to the agnostic, and our personal adventures before and after make clear three pertinent ideas:

a. That we were alcoholic and could not manage our own lives.

b. That probably no human power could have relieved our alcoholism.

c. That God could and would if He were sought.

Reprinted with permission

The Twelve Traditions

These are for groups, to help groups of alcoholics to work together to carry its message to the alcoholic who still suffers

1. Our common welfare should come first; personal recovery depends upon A.A. unity.

2. For our group purpose there is but one ultimate authority--a loving God as He may express Himself in our group con-science. Our leaders are but trusted servants; they do not govern.

3. The only requirement for A.A. membership is a desire to stop drinking.

4. Each group should be autonomous except in matters affecting other groups or A.A. as a whole.

5. Each group has but one primary purpose--to carry its message to the alcoholic who still suffers.

6. An A.A. group ought never endorse, finance, or lend the A.A. name to any related facility or

outside enterprise, lest problems of money, property, and prestige divert us from our primary purpose.

7. Every A.A. group ought to be fully self-supporting, declining outside contributions.

8. Alcoholics Anonymous should remain forever non-professional, but our service centers may employ special workers.

9. A.A., as such, ought never be organized; but we may create service boards or committees directly responsible to those they serve.

10. Alcoholics Anonymous has no opinion on outside issues; hence the A.A. name ought never be drawn into public controversy.

11. Our public relations policy is based on attraction rather than promotion; we need always maintain personal anonymity at the level of press, radio, and films.

12. Anonymity is the spiritual foundation of all our traditions, ever reminding us to place principles before personalities.

Reprinted with permission

The Promises

These paragraphs are from the end of step nine in the book <u>Alcoholics Anonymous</u> and reflect a reasonable set of expectations for this phase of the program (end of ninth step)

If we are painstaking about this phase of our development, we will be amazed before we are halfway through. We are going to know a new freedom and a new happiness. We will not regret the past nor wish to shut the door on it. We will comprehend the word serenity and we will know peace. No matter how far down the scale we have gone, we will see how our experience can benefit others. The feeling of uselessness and self-pity will disappear. We will lose interest in selfish things and gain interest in our fellows. Self-seeking will slip away. Our whole attitude and outlook upon life will change. Fear of people and of economic insecurity will leave us. We will intuitively know how to handle situations which used to baffle us. We will suddenly realize that God is doing for us what we could not do for ourselves.

Are these extravagant promises? We think not. They are being fulfilled among us — sometimes quickly, sometimes slowly. They will always materialize if we work for them.

Reprinted with permission

A Vision for You

This quote is from the end of <u>Alcoholics Anonymous</u> Chapter 11, the end of the basic instructions contained in the first 164 pages

Our book is meant to be suggestive only. We realize we know only a little. God will constantly disclose more to you and to us. Ask Him in your morning meditation what you can do each day for the man who is still sick. The answers will come, if your own house is in order.

But obviously you cannot transmit something you haven't got. See to it that your relationship with Him is right, and great events will come to pass for you and countless others. This is the Great Fact for us.

Abandon yourself to God as you understand God. Admit your faults to Him and to your fellows. Clear away the wreckage of your past. Give freely of what you find and join us. We shall be with you in the Fellowship of the Spirit, and you will surely meet some of us as you trudge the Road of Happy Destiny.

May God bless you and keep you until then.

Reprinted with permission

Ideas for Prayers

Meetings often start and/or end with prayers, and they often make for a good topic

Serenity Prayer

God grant me

The serenity to accept the things I cannot change

The courage to change the things I can and

The wisdom to know the difference

Third Step Prayer (modified)

God, [Creative Intelligence, Universal Mind, Spirit of Nature or Spirit of the Universe]

I offer myself to Thee--to build with me and to do with me as Thou wilt.

Relieve me of the bondage of self, that I may better do Thy will.

Take away my difficulties, that victory over them may bear witness to those I would help of Thy Power, Thy Love, and Thy Way of life.

May I do Thy will always!

Seventh Step Prayer (modified)

My Creator [Creative Intelligence, Universal Mind, Spirit of Nature or Spirit of the Universe], I am now willing that you should have all of me, good and bad. I pray that you now remove from me every single defect of character which stands in the way of my usefulness to you and my fellows. Grant me strength, as I go out from here, to do your bidding.

Peace Prayer or Saint Francis Prayer

Lord, make me an instrument of your peace.

Where there is hatred, let me bring love.

Where there is offence, let me bring pardon.

Where there is discord, let me bring union.

Where there is error, let me bring truth.

Where there is doubt, let me bring faith.

Where there is despair, let me bring hope.

Where there is darkness, let me bring your light.

Where there is sadness, let me bring joy.

O' Master, let me not seek as much to be consoled as to console, to be understood as to understand, to be loved as to love, for it is in giving that one receives, it is in self-forgetting that one finds, it is in pardoning that one is pardoned, it is in dying that one is raised to eternal life.

Ideas for Meeting Topics

There are ten times more topics for meetings than there are people at the meeting, but it becomes hard to think of one on the spot. This list is really to spark your thought process rather than limit your imagination

One important suggestion is that very private subjects (i.e. sex details and politics) are better suited for private discussion one on one with a sponsor or other close recovery buddy. Any actual criminal activity should not be discussed outside of legal and clerical settings. There is no privileged information outside of clergy or lawyers, most especially at an open recovery meeting.

Amends

Anger

Any one of the Twelve Steps

Any one of the Twelve Traditions

Being helpful?

Credit where credit is due

Cruel words or actions

Dishonesty

Ego

Fear

Giving myself credit for accomplishments

Good intentions, bad result

Good results imperfect intentions

Gratitude

Growth

Harsh words or actions

How can I do for others?

How do I do for others?

How long should it take to finish the steps?

How many meetings do I need?

Kindness

Love

Loving one's self

My past as a tool to help others

-What it was like

-What happened

-What it is like now

(half of the time on the first two, the other half of the time on the last)

Packing the stream of life?

Prayer

Progress not perfection

Religion

Resentment

Secrets

Self-seeking

Selfishness

Short versions of

Spirituality

Sponsorship

Thinking only of me

Thinking only of others

What could I do better?

What is a good sponsor?

Big Book Index

This list is from the book <u>Alcoholics Anonymous</u>, second edition and you can get a free pdf download many places online. You will likely own a third or fourth edition of <u>Alcoholics Anonymous</u>, but you'll be close. Here is a fair list of pages that mention words associated with many issues we face and make great meeting topic reading

Terms, Definitions & Explanations

AA, and recovery in general, has a language all of its own, most of this one learns in context during meetings. Here are some thoughts and musings on the meanings of things you may hear. This section, like everything in this booklet, is not 'all encompassing' nor is it absolute, just a start and useful to help newcomers to AA

7th tradition -- Meetings are self-supportive and rely on donations from members to pay for expenses such as rent. Whatever is passed around is often called 'the basket' or 'the hat' it is customary to donate a dollar or two

12 concepts -- Principles to guide AA's General Service Board and the General Service Conference which are the primary way AA relates to the world.

12 steps -- The heart of the AA program the twelve steps intended to be worked with another person (see 'sponsor' below)

12 traditions -- Foundational set of principles to guide relationships between groups and between groups and individual members.

anniversary -- Members are asked to share their sobriety milestones of 1 month, 2 months, 3 months, etc. up to a year and then full years. Customs vary greatly among groups and geographic areas (see chips and tokens)

anonymity -- AA is based on personal anonymous, at a public level of media--each AA has a perspective on the tradition of anonymity, but a minimum is often not using one's full name in any widely public medium to express opinions and information about Alcoholics Anonymous. Our own sobriety separated from AA is our own business to share or not share

autonomy -- groups are independent entities, they share a common purpose and often follow AA Traditions, the idea that the group decides how it works is a tradition itself (the fourth)

big book -- The book <u>Alcoholics Anonymous</u>, which describes the 12 step program and describes how one can recover from alcoholism

burning desire -- Usually, at the end of the meeting, the chair asks if anyone has a burning desire to share, or to use or drink or harm themselves or others.

chair -- Service position (volunteer), filled by an AA member, that helps keep the group's administration together. Not really needed for impromptu meetings

chips or tokens -- Members receive coins, tokens or just acknowledgment to mark milestones such as 90 days or years of sobriety at least in part to show to newcomers long term sobriety can be done (see anniversary)

crosstalk -- Crosstalk is giving advice, questioning, interrupting, or speaking directly to another person rather than to the group. It is frowned upon at most meetings

fellowship -- A term for the society of AA

group -- Set of meetings that happen on a recurring basis

home group -- Meeting that an AA member attends on a weekly/recurring basis and where one participates in the Group Conscience on matters outside the group. Really, one has a single home group although which one may change from time to time

leader-- A person who starts the discussion, often with sharing and a topic (the topic is often ignored by the members, they will share what is important to them, roll with it)

member -- The only requirement for AA membership is a desire to stop drinking, groups sometimes have added requirements and their rules are their rules, nothing written here changes that

sponsor -- An AA member who serves as a mentor to a newcomer or another member in the program this usually includes 'working the steps' together

Links

Search for AA Intergroup and follow the link to your nearest Intergroup where you can find all kinds of resources including lists of local and zoom meetings

US and Canada AA --> AA Intergroups

International directory of AA (PDF) --> GSO, CO, IG and Answering Services

Online Intergroup --> https://aa-intergroup.org

Alcoholics Anonymous World Service --> www.aa.org

P.O. Box 459, Grand Central Station

New York, NY 10163 (212) 870-3400

Second edition of the book Alcoholics Anonymous. This is in the public domain which means the copyright expired and anyone can down load it free. This is one, there are others.

https://www.12step.org/docs/BigBook.pdf

Author's contact

zentoid.master@gmail.com

Virtual Meetings

Virtual meetings are likely a forever thing. Some may have started because of the COVID 19 Pandemic, but many virtual meetings will continue and will be started as the world moves on from COVID 19. It is another way to have online meetings which have been around for many years. These are, as is everything in else in E-Pocket Meeting, general ideas and enough specifics to just do it on Zoom™ or a Zoom™-type platform

Virtual Meeting Admin Duties

- Do not read the following, but the organizer/secretary/Virtual Meeting Admin is responsible for performing these items:

- Arrive early to setup the 'Breakout Rooms'

- Create half a dozen rooms, Zoom™ does not allow more breakout rooms after starting (as of this writing)

- Rename breakout room #1 as "The Meeting Room"

- Rename breakout room #2 as "Information and Literature"

- Start the breakout rooms

- Assign members 'The Meeting Room'

- Go to the meeting portal to greet and chat with guests before inviting them to 'The Meeting Room'--provide instructions if they are unfamiliar with 'Breakout Rooms'

- Make at least the Secretary a Co-Host, so they can help manage the meeting. Do this before putting them into the The Meeting Room

- Mute mics on entering 'The Meeting Room'

- Be helpful, if you notice members struggling with mute or unmute – Help

- Find out phone users names and rename them to first name, this is a Zoom Bomber prevention tool

- If harassment starts on the chat, disable it for the harasser and maybe remove them from the Meeting Room

- Watch for 'Zoom Bombers' (malicious or disruptive individuals) read the instructions below (maybe print them so they are right in front of you), do the minimum to get the attack under control, but get it under control

* Note: Only use the "On Hold" and "Lock Meeting" options briefly as they can stop late arriving members or newcomers from getting into the meeting.

Secretary Format addition:

Our Virtual Meeting Admin has created a breakout room for any newcomers and anyone who would like to get more information about this meeting or other meetings, wants to find out about getting AA literature, or has questions about sponsorship. The Information and Literature breakout room will be available immediately after the meeting closes. If you would like to ask questions, private message our Virtual Meeting Admin, _____, to ask to be added to that room.

Virtual Meeting Admin Announcement

<u>When called on by the leader or secretary, read the following:</u>

- Hi, my name is _____, and I am an alcoholic, and I am the Virtual Meeting Admin.

- To maintain anonymity, all Zoom recording options are disabled. Please do not record, photograph, or republish any part of this meeting.

- Please mute your microphone when you are not reading or sharing.

- As the chat feature can be used for harassment, please send me a private chat if you feel you are being harassed and I can stop it.

- There will be an 'Information and Literature' breakout room after the meeting for who have questions about the meeting, AA literature, sponsorship, or about AA in general.

Near the end of the meeting use chat to send this message to everyone

Got questions? There will be an 'Information and Literature' breakout room after the meeting for who have questions about the meeting, AA literature, sponsorship, or about AA in general. Send me a private chat to me and I'll give you access and arrange for couple of group members to be available in the room for 5 minutes or so after the meeting.

Note: If a new person asks for this, ask two other members to help staff that room. Send two of the volunteers a personal chat message. If not pre-arranged ask for volunteers.

Zoom Bomber Plan

Using the Participants window controls, perform the following steps, in this order:

1. Disable "Allow Participants to Unmute Themselves."

2. Mute All

3. Unmute Speaker

4. Disable "Allow Participants to Rename Themselves"

5. Lock meeting

6. Remove the bombers from the meeting

7. Unlock the meeting

Acknowledgement

Alcoholics Anonymous, both the book and the movement, is the story of how many millions of men and women have recovered from alcoholism. Many owe their lives to AA, as do I

Author Bio

Ray has been sober for nearly three decades practicing the principles of Alcoholics Anonymous. He has traveled the world both in the U.S. Navy and as a civilian for work and pleasure. Since retiring he and his bride have traveled the United States seeing the National Parks and Forests and each of the lower forty-eight states. He considers this life a gift of remaining sober and practicing the principles taught to him in the rooms of Alcoholics Anonymous.

~ ~

Made in United States
Orlando, FL
12 March 2023

30976284R00024